Fantastic Fairy Tales

Donna Freitag

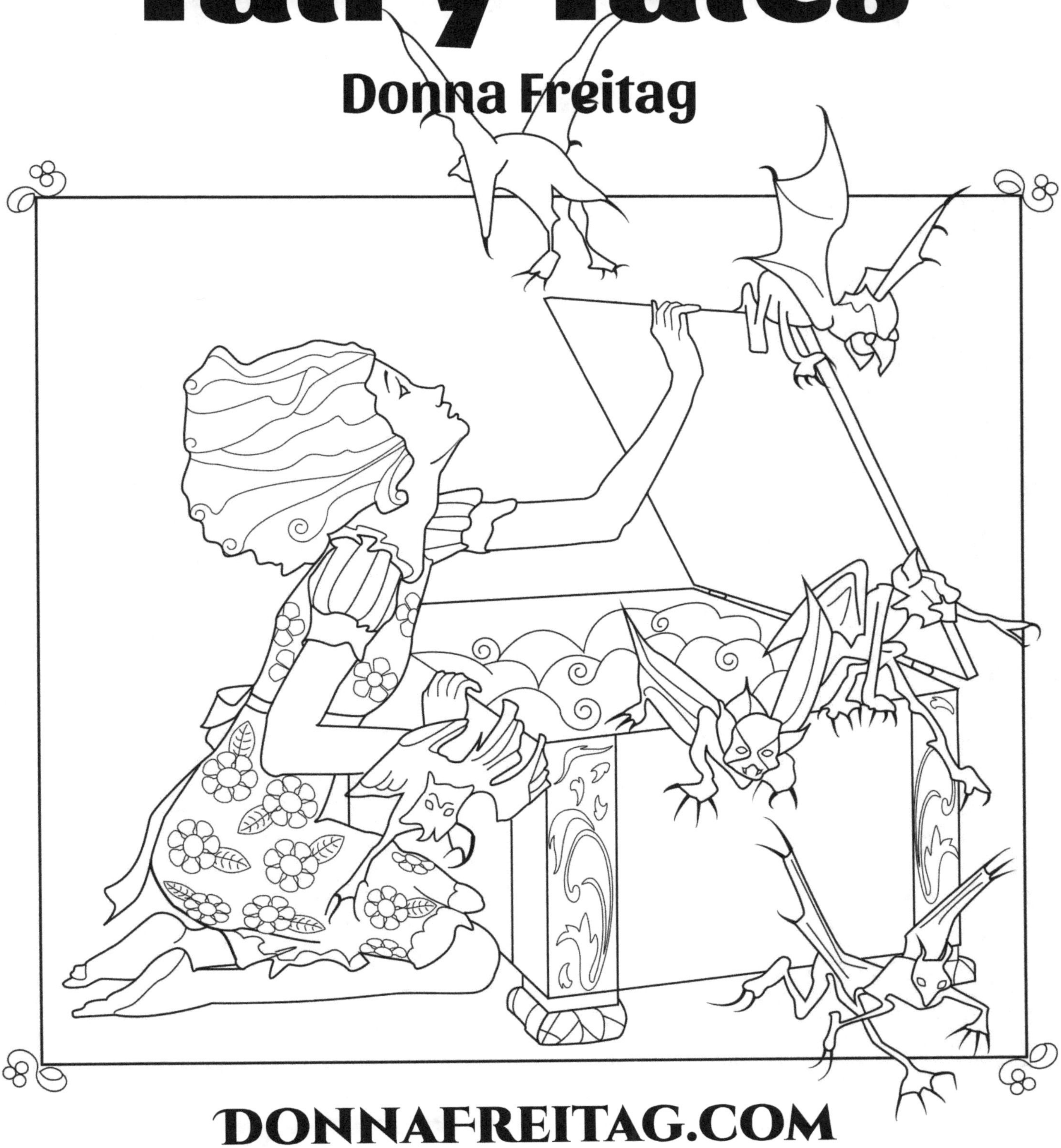

DONNAFREITAG.COM

How to color this book

Fantastic Fairy Tales is a coloring book for adults. You'll enjoy hours of creative, relaxing, stress relieving fun as you color 25 all new space age designs. All are beautiful, new, original artwork never before seen in any collection.

Coloring Tips

Colored pencils are the most popular way to color. It's best to get a large set of at least 48 colors. Some of the best brands are Prismacolor and Staedtler.

In addition, you'll need an eraser and a good pencil sharpener. Also popular are markers. Warning: they tend to bleed through the page. So if you use them, place a sheet or thick paper underneath so the ink doesn't leak onto the picture below. Copic markers are a great brand.

Marker sets offer a smaller choice of colors than pencil sets. That's one reason why the pro colorists often use a combination of pencils, markers, gel pens and even crayons.

It all depends on the effects you want to produce.

Please post photos of your artwork on my Facebook page. I'd love to see what you've done!

Be sure to follow us on social media...

f donnafreitag90

t @donna_r_freitag

ig @donnafreitag1991

p donna_freitag

Join our mailing list for the latest news and freebies.

Visit www.donnafreitag.com

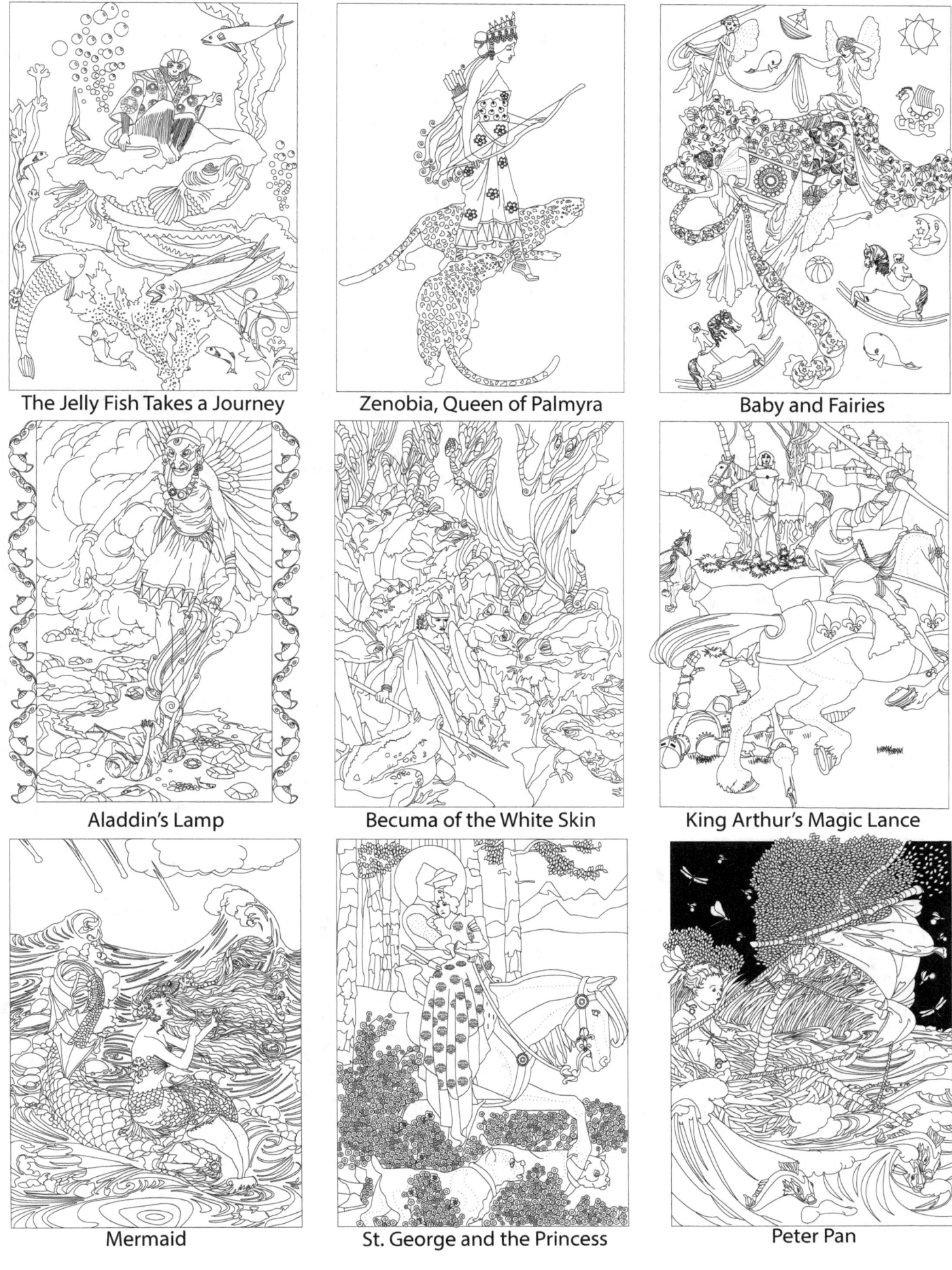

The Jelly Fish Takes a Journey

Zenobia, Queen of Palmyra

Baby and Fairies

Aladdin's Lamp

Becuma of the White Skin

King Arthur's Magic Lance

Mermaid

St. George and the Princess

Peter Pan

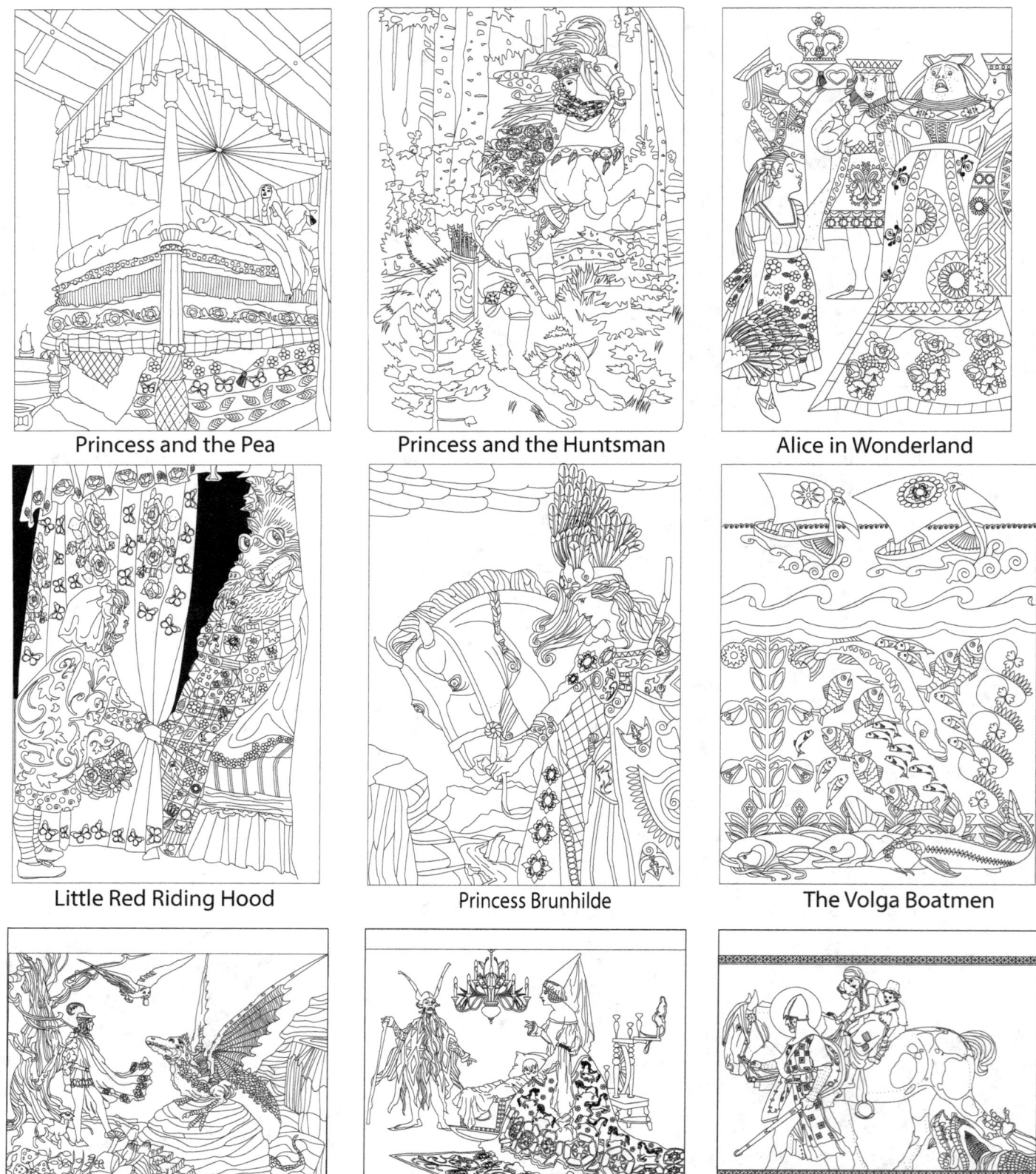

Princess and the Pea

Princess and the Huntsman

Alice in Wonderland

Little Red Riding Hood

Princess Brunhilde

The Volga Boatmen

Prince Charming

Rumpelstilskin

St. George and the Dragon

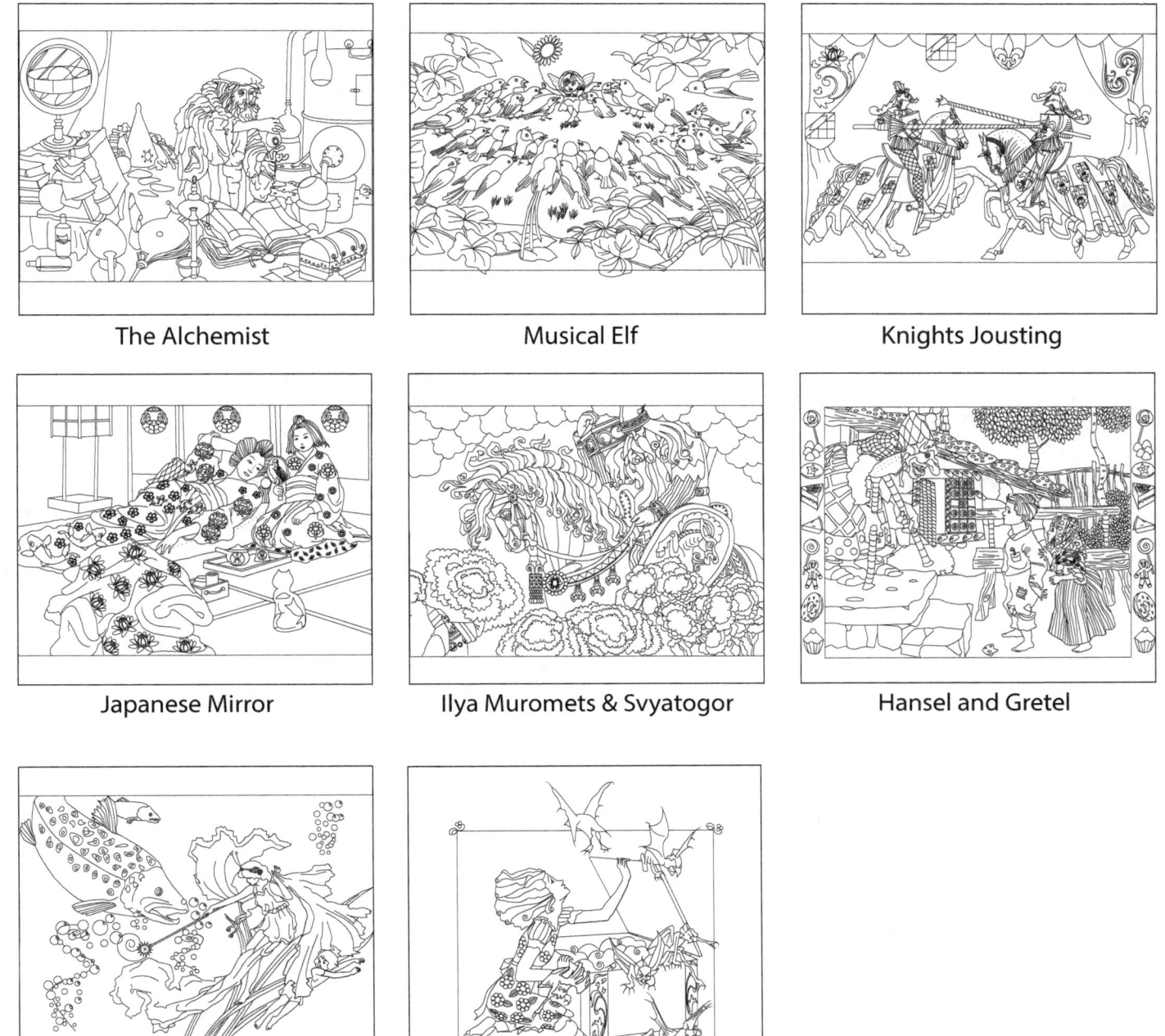

The Alchemist

Musical Elf

Knights Jousting

Japanese Mirror

Ilya Muromets & Svyatogor

Hansel and Gretel

Fairies in the Fish Pond

Pandora's Box

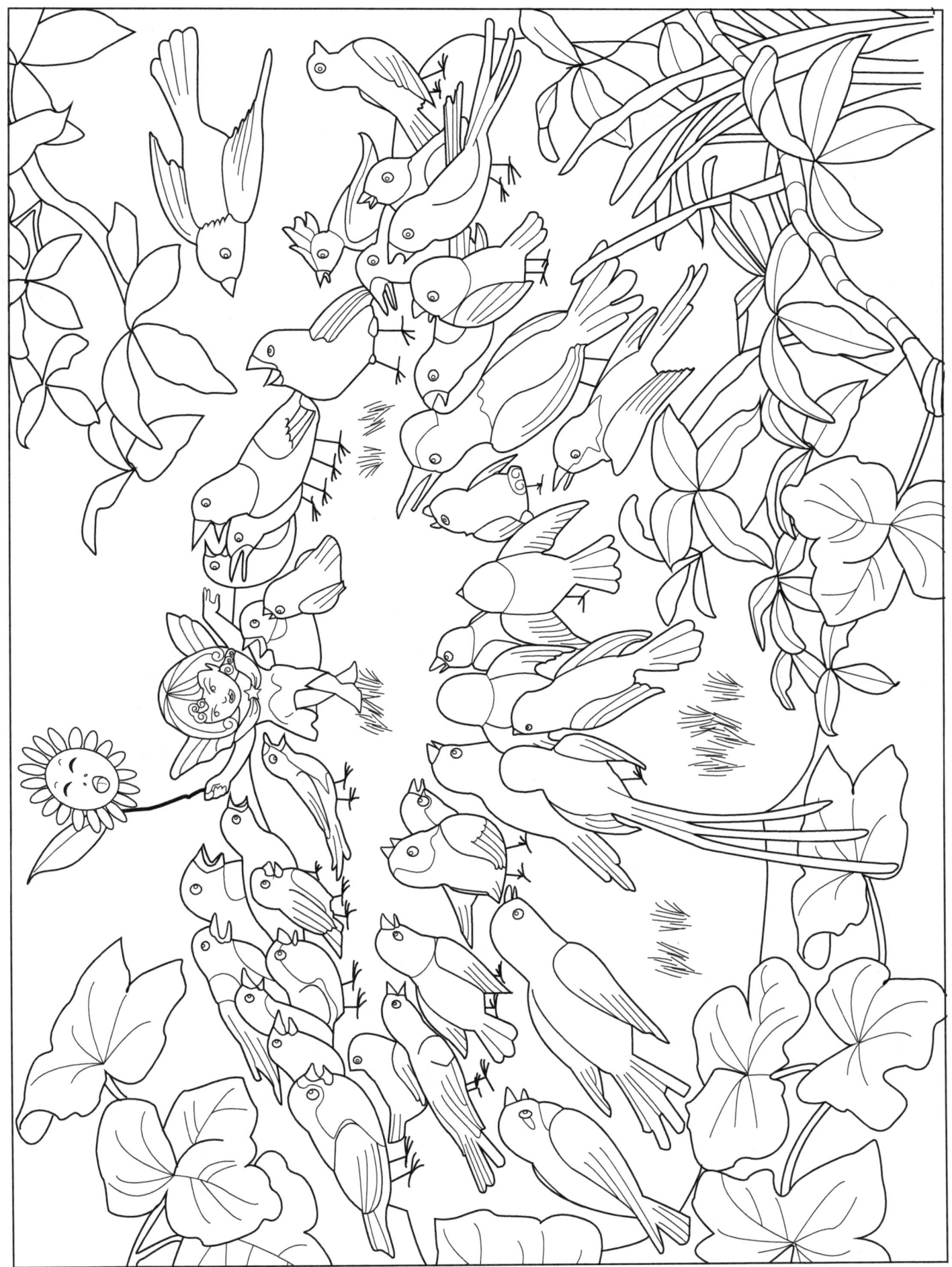

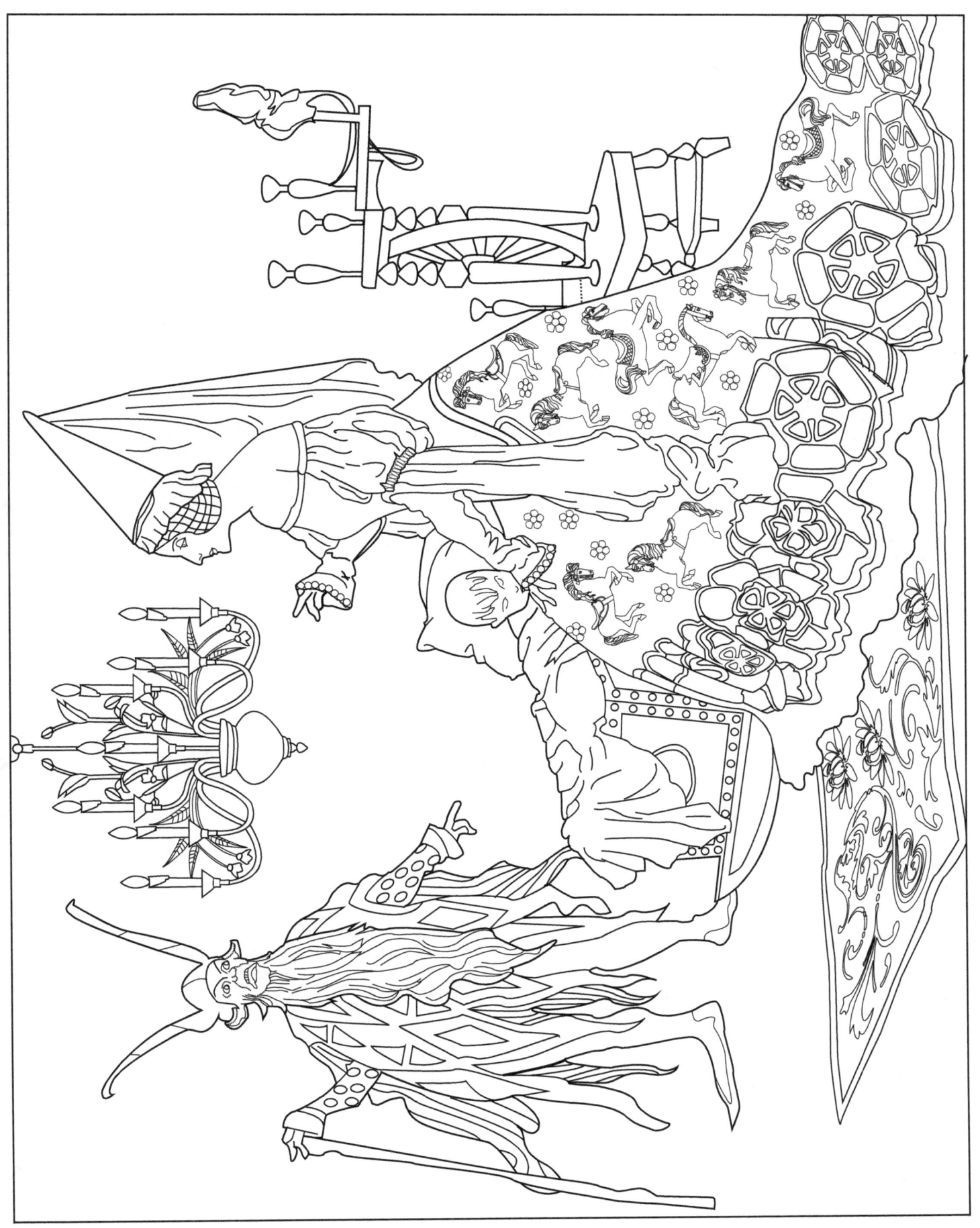

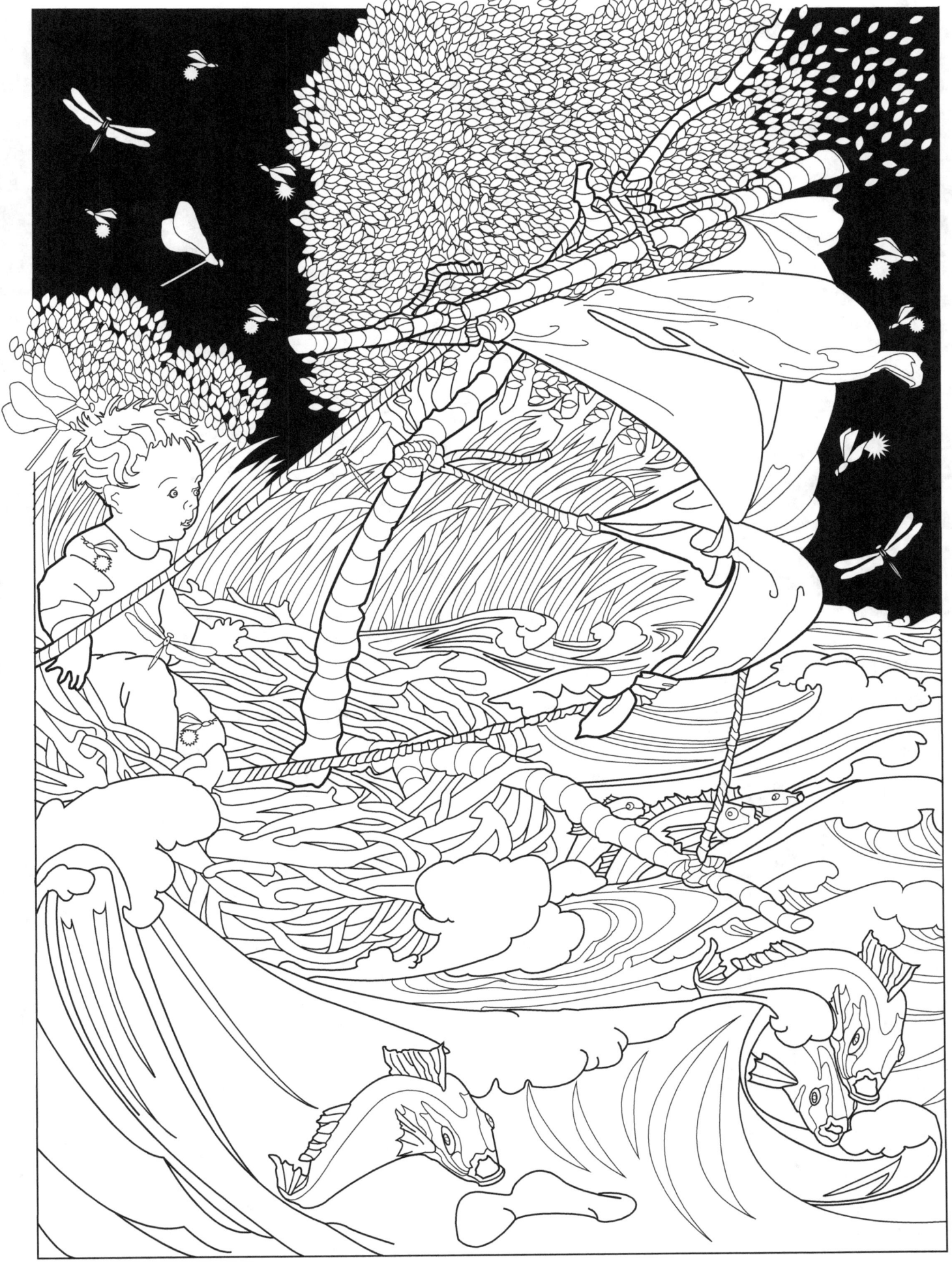

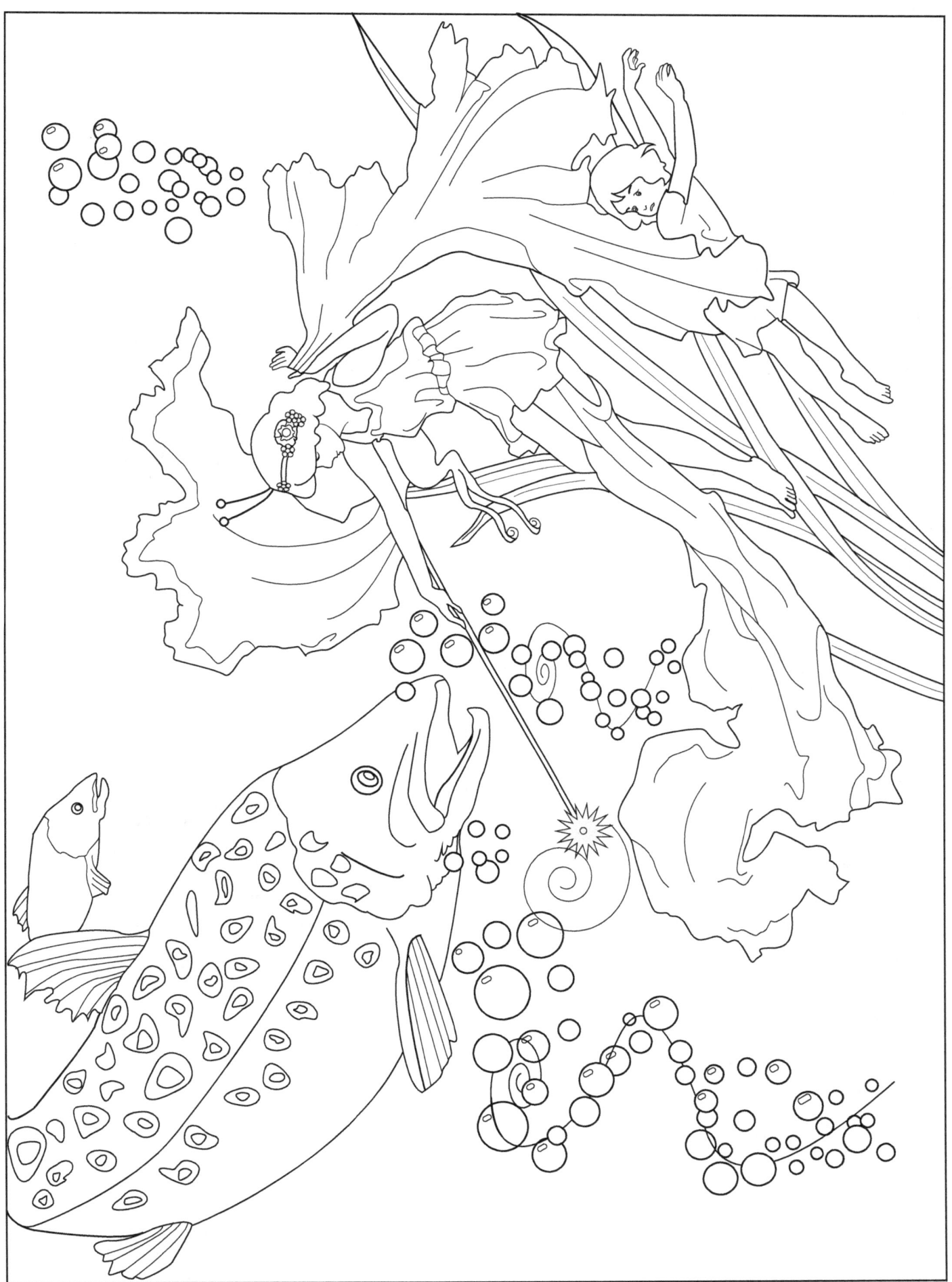

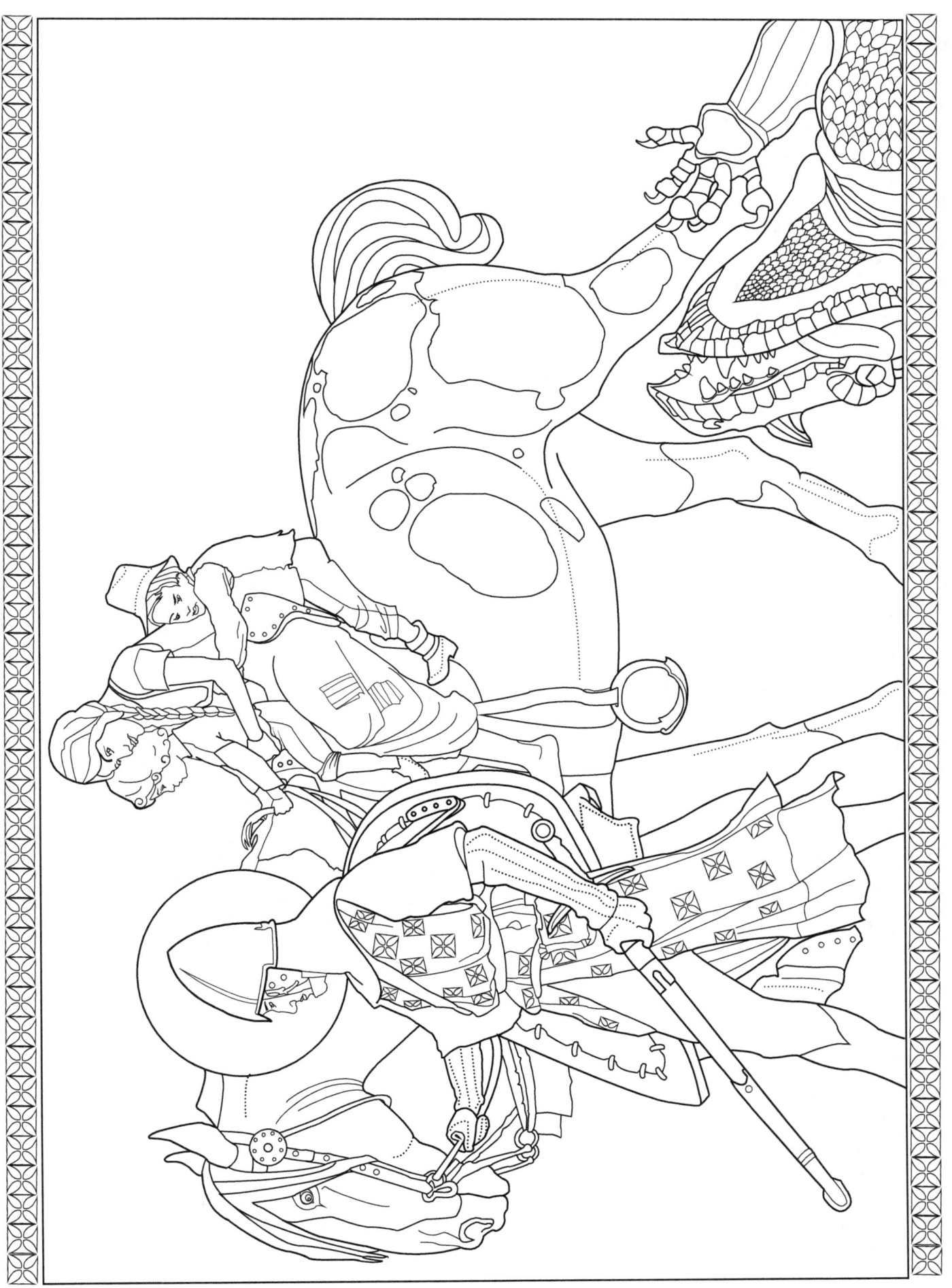

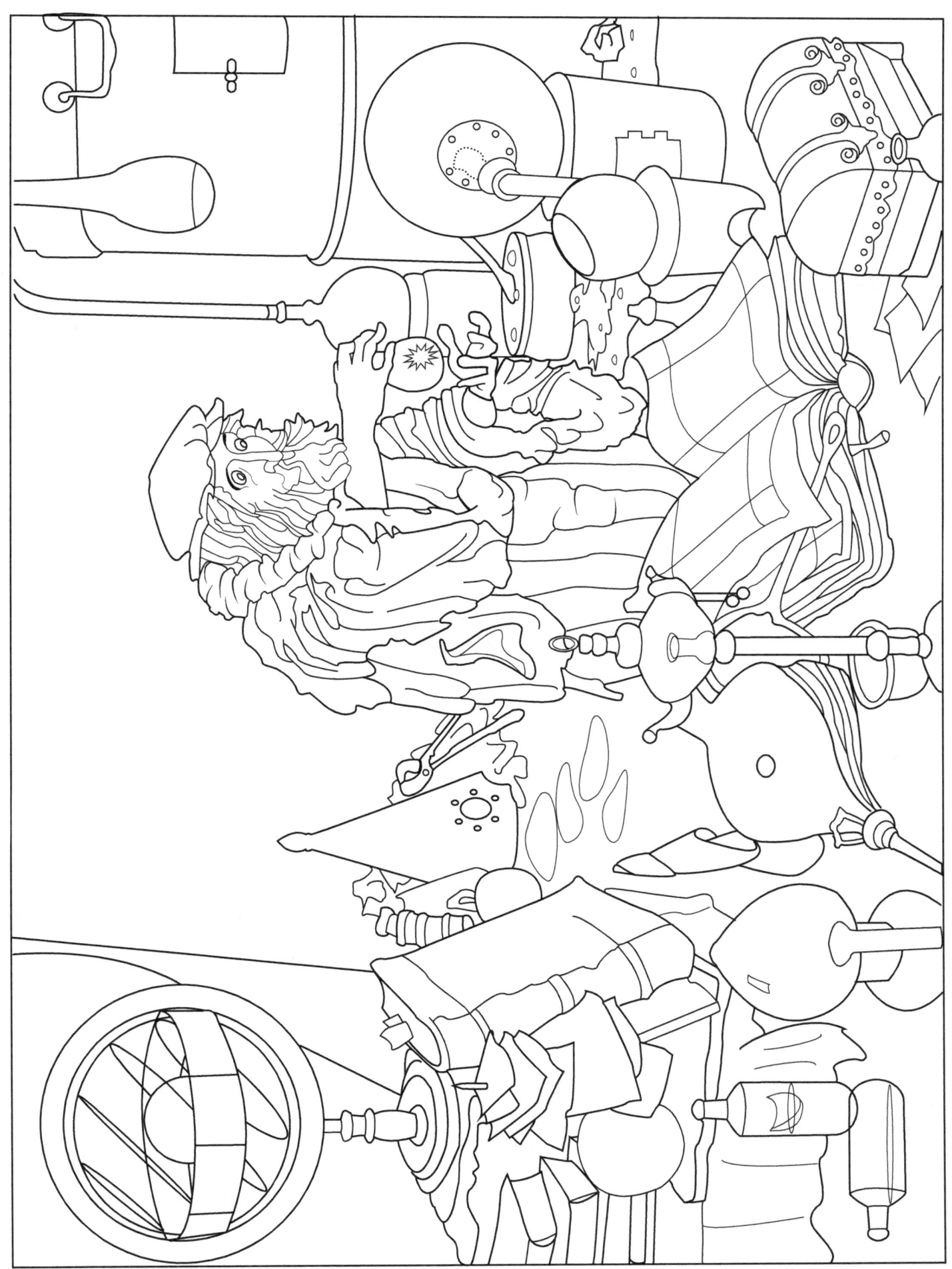

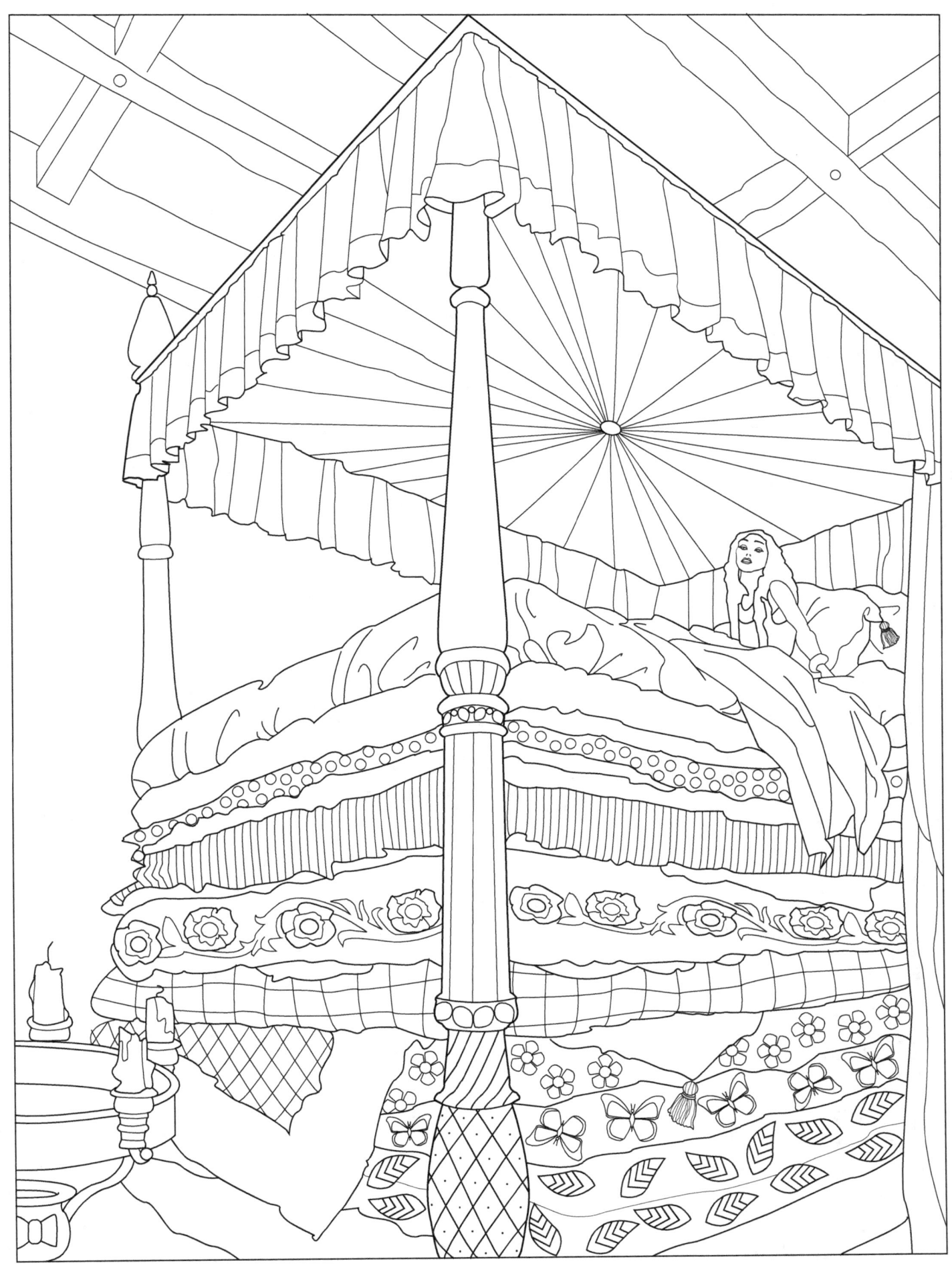

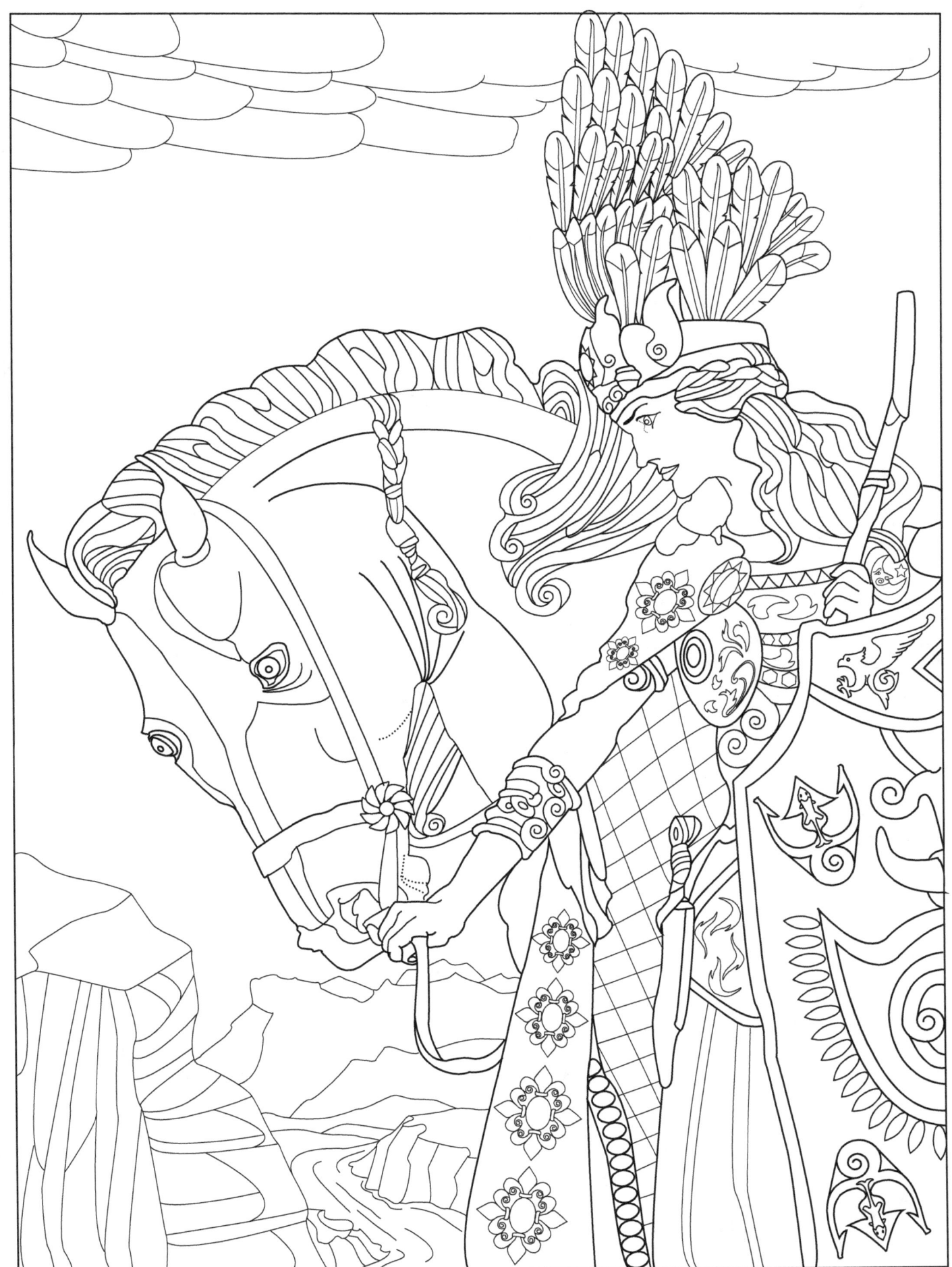

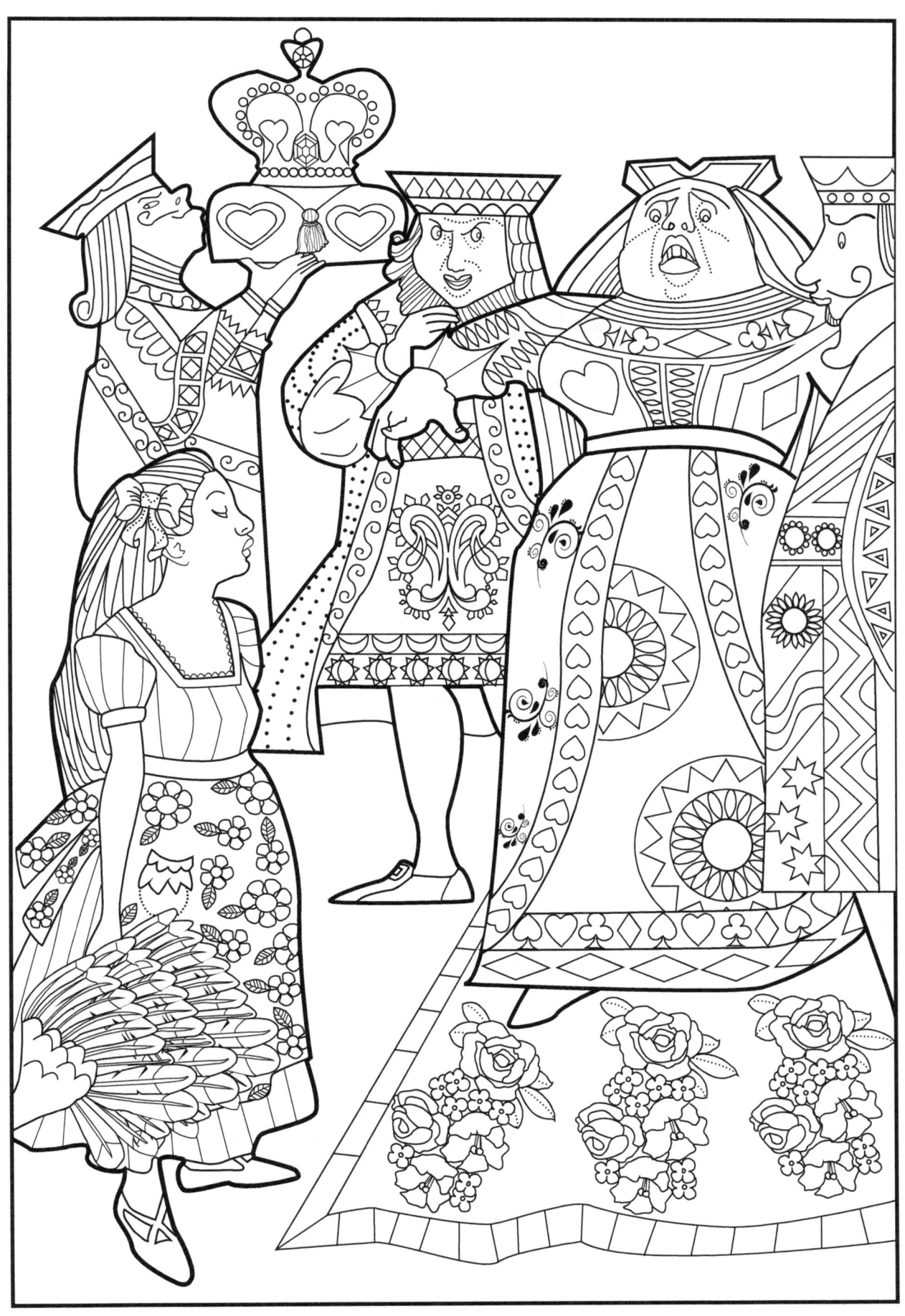

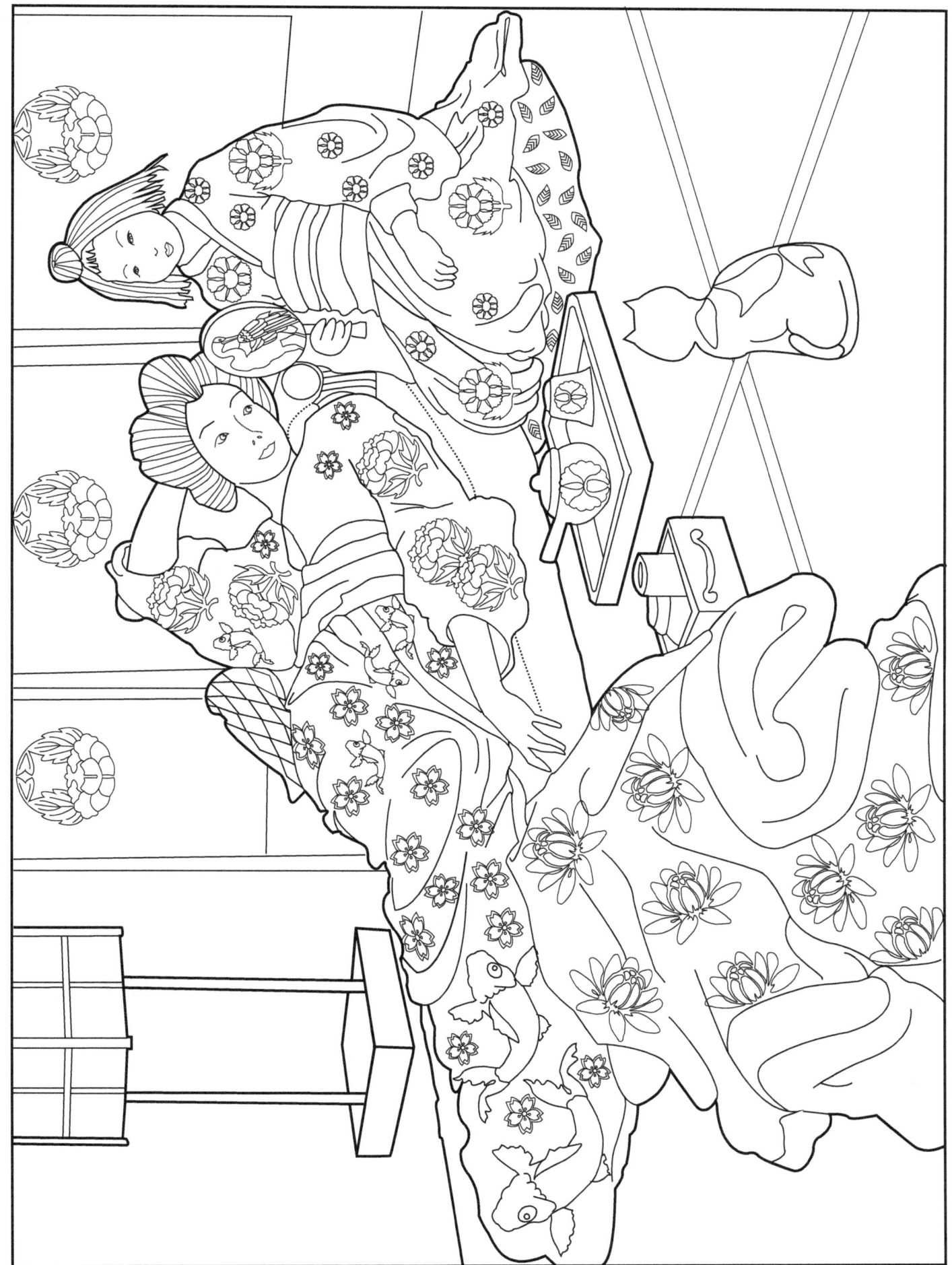

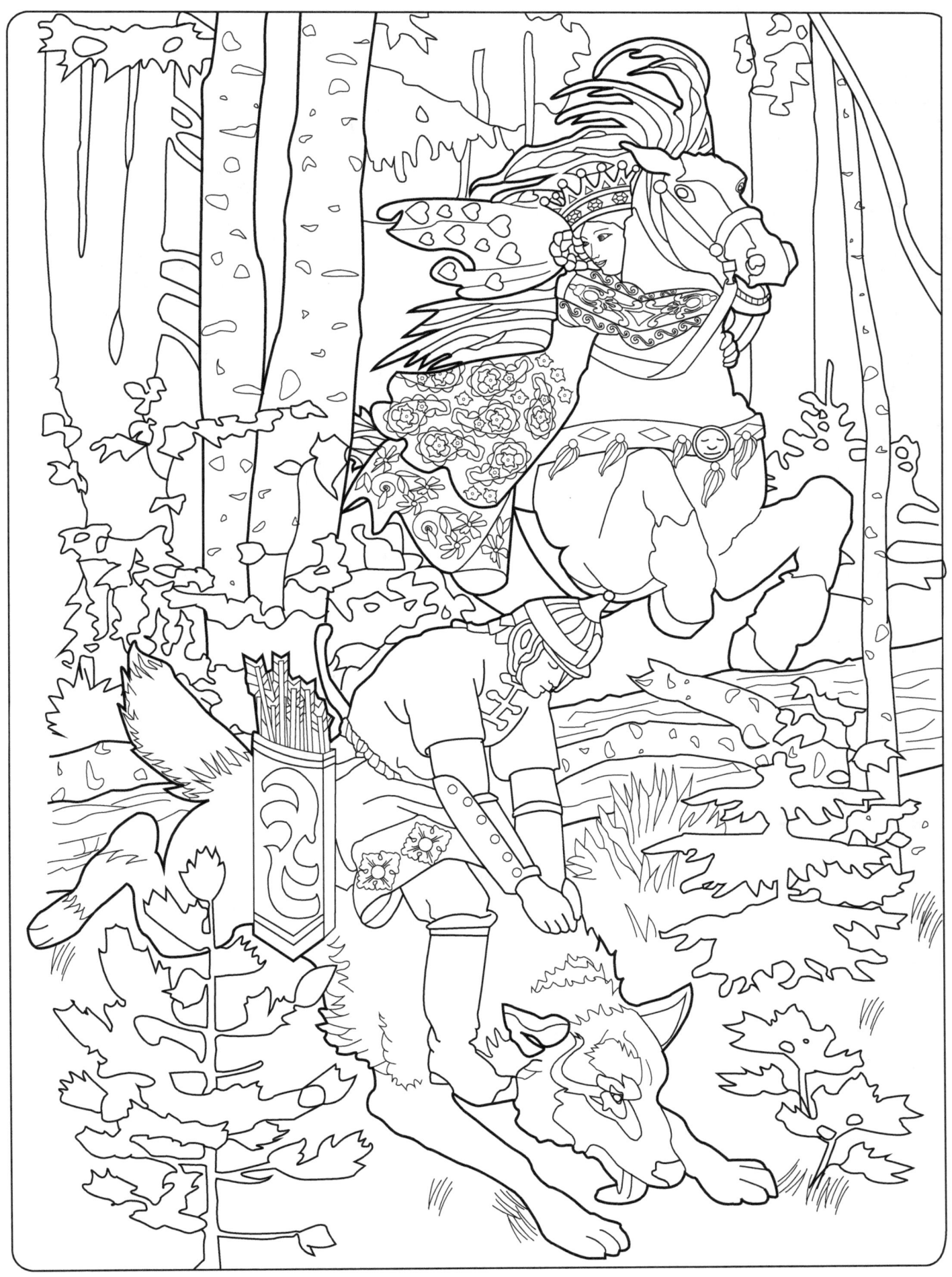

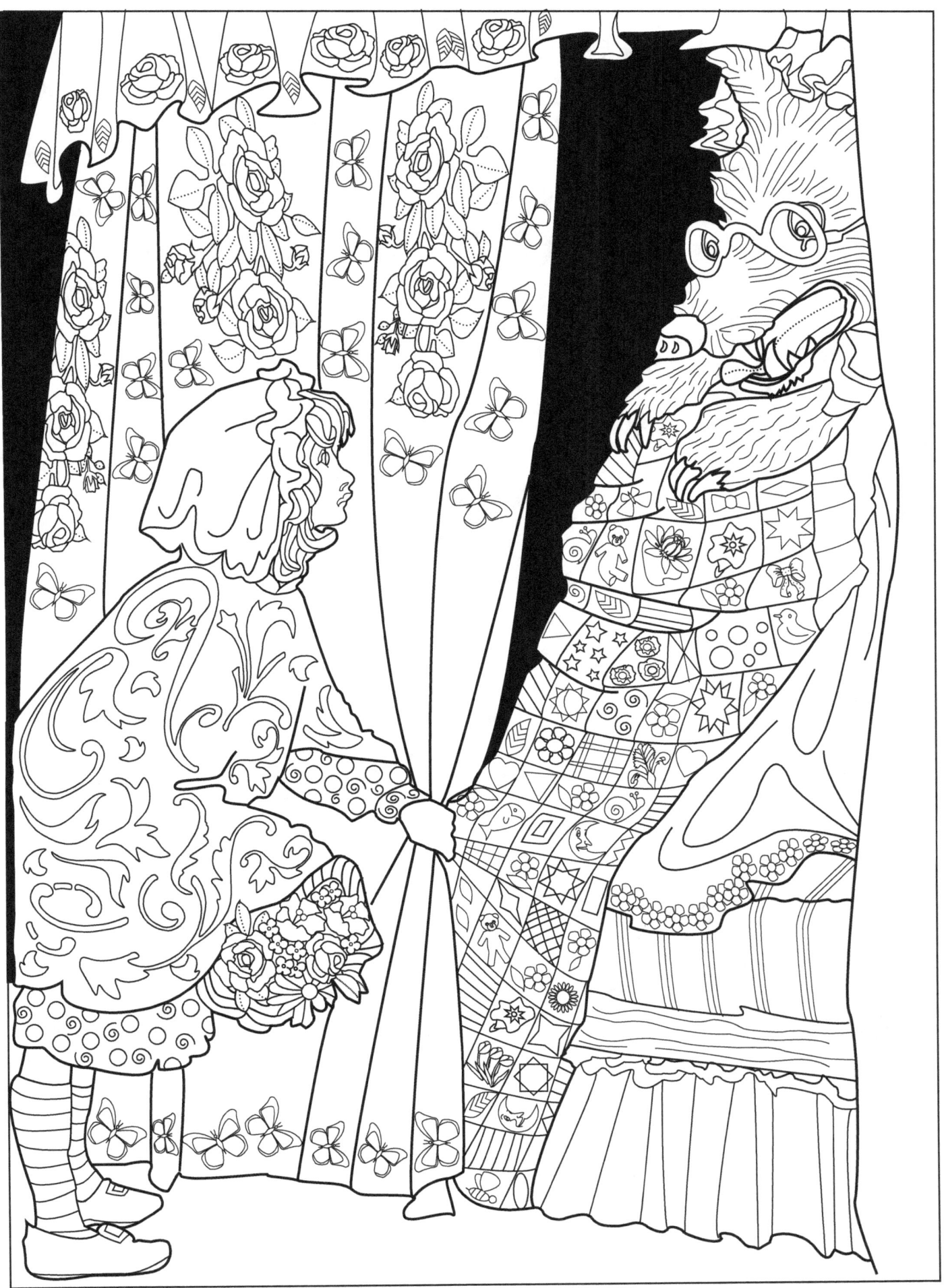

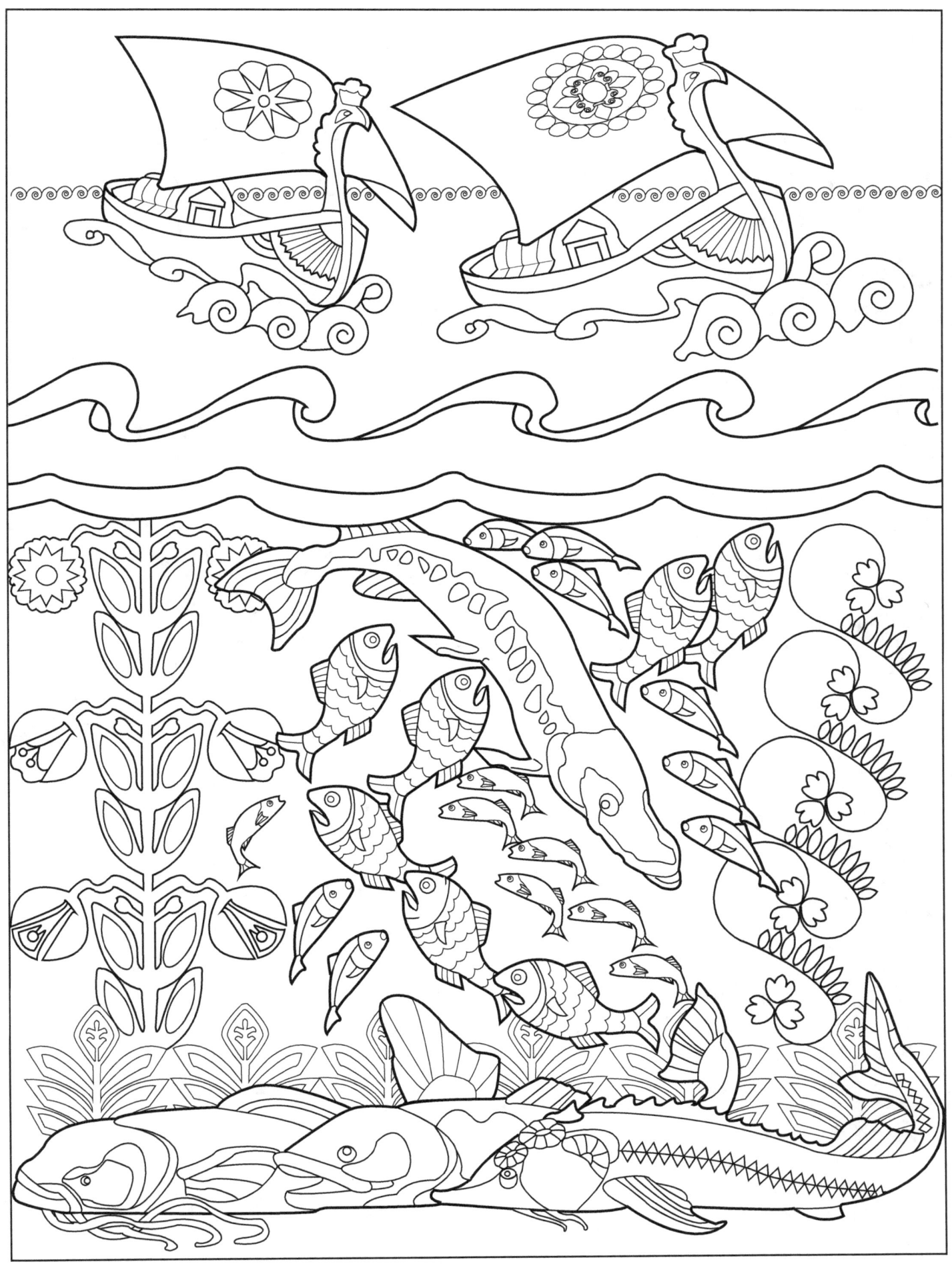

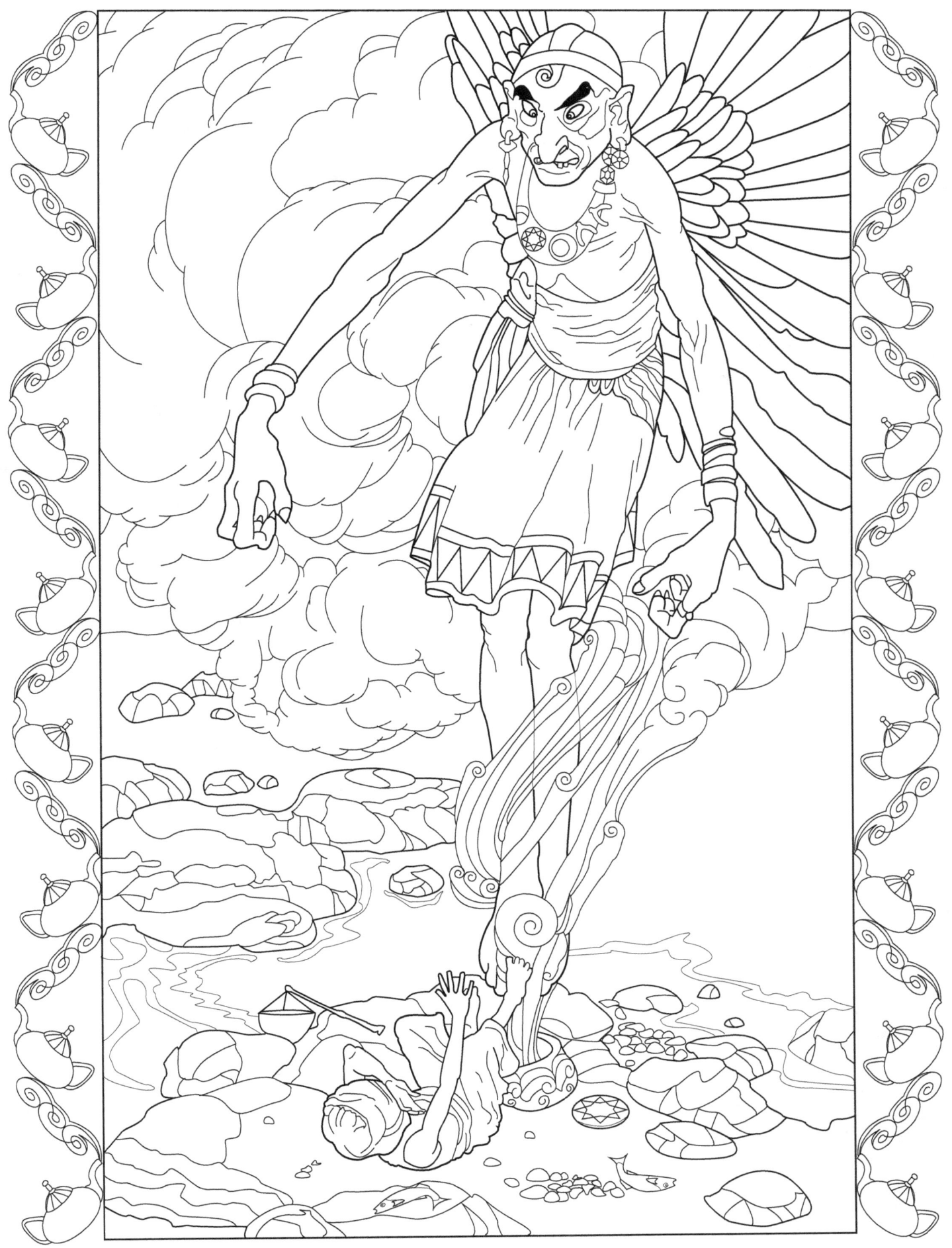

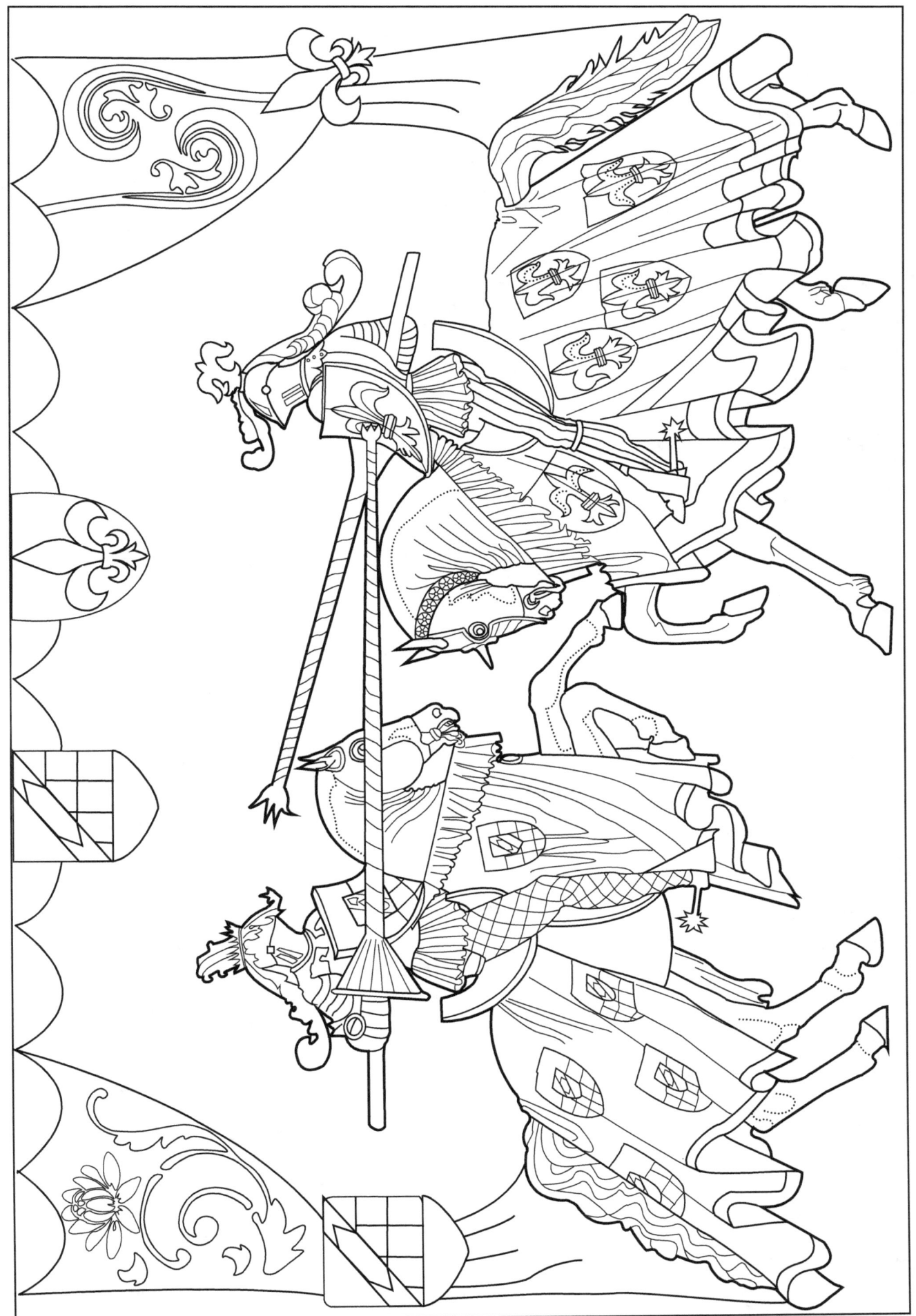

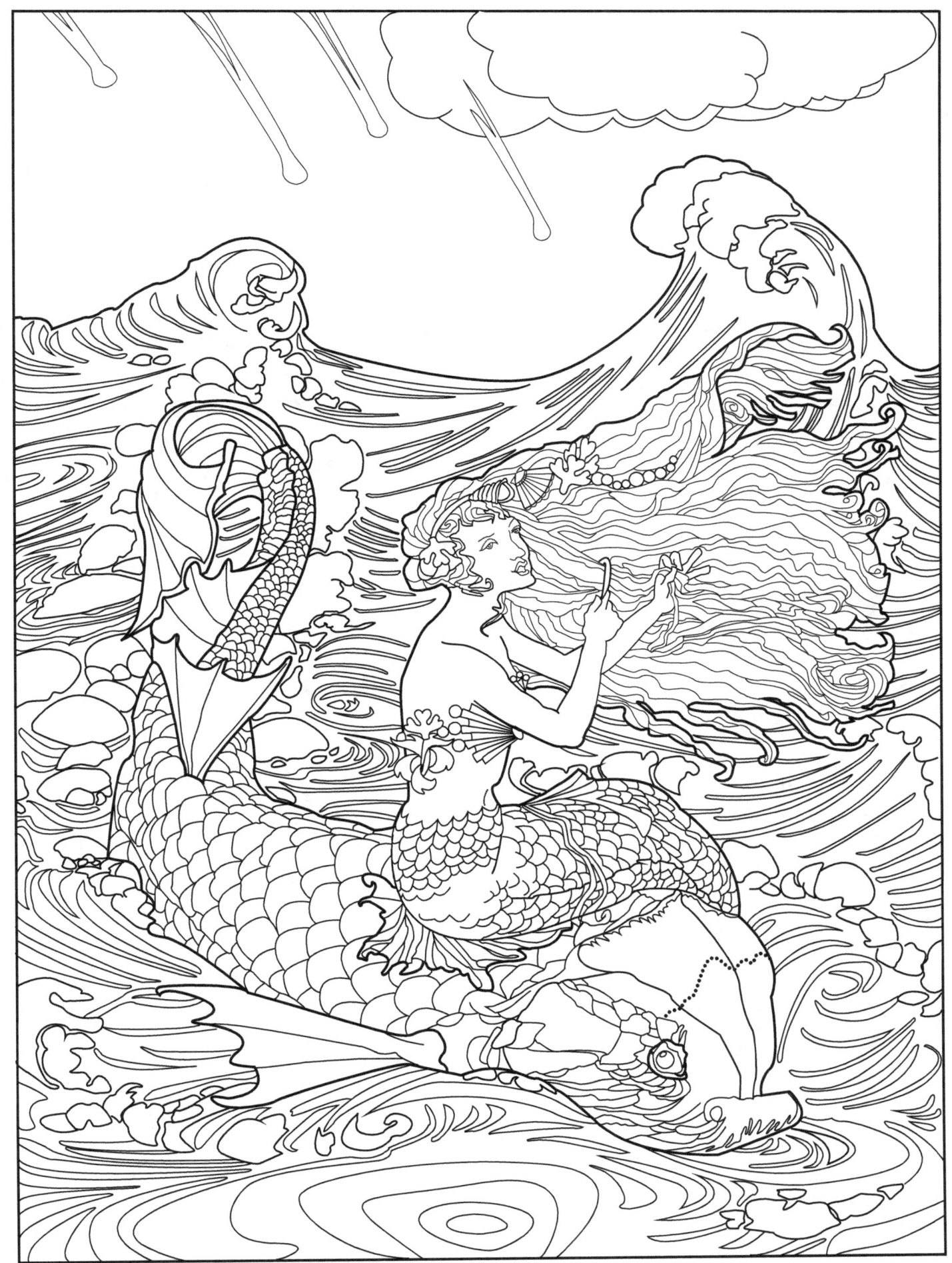

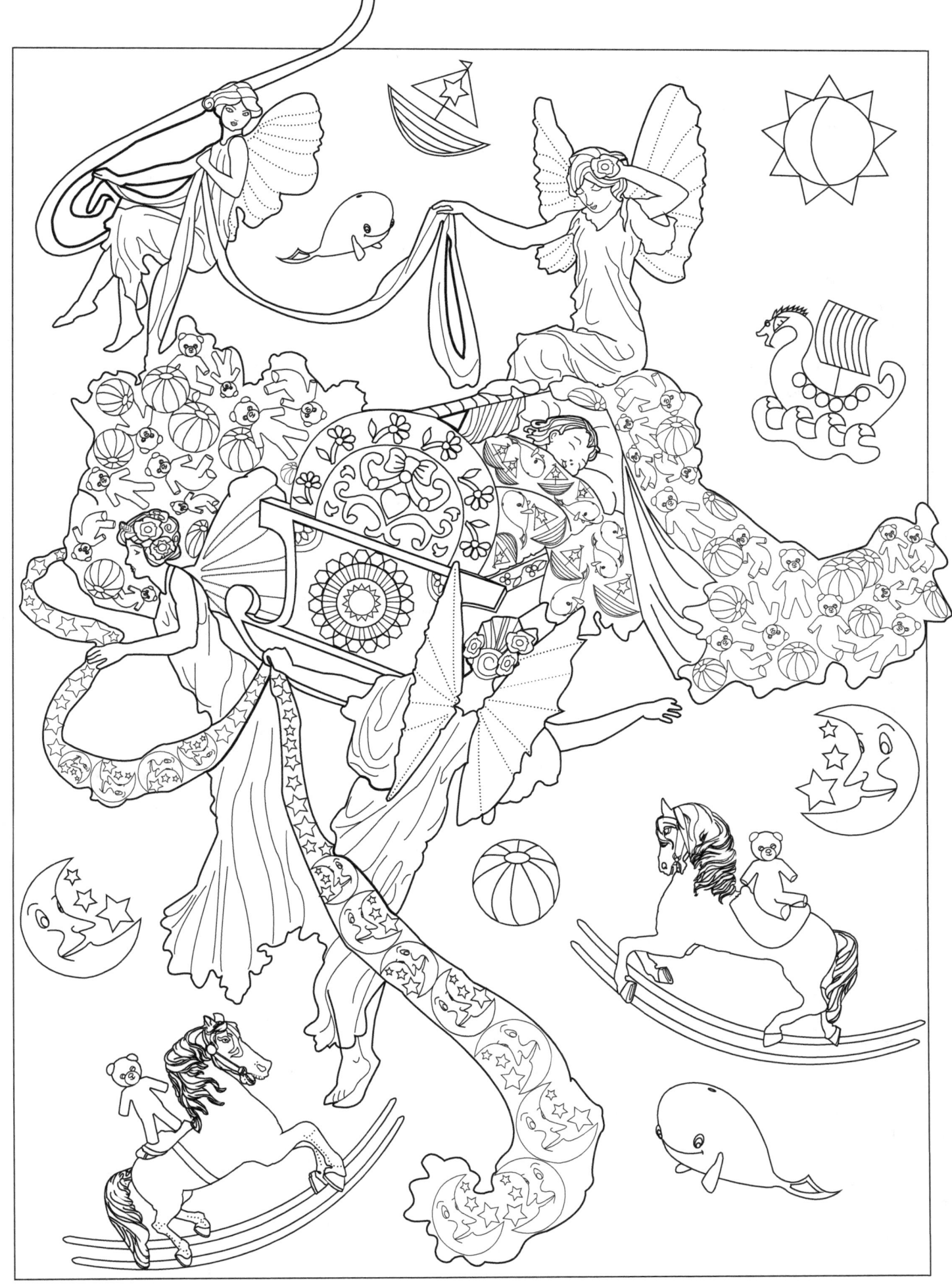

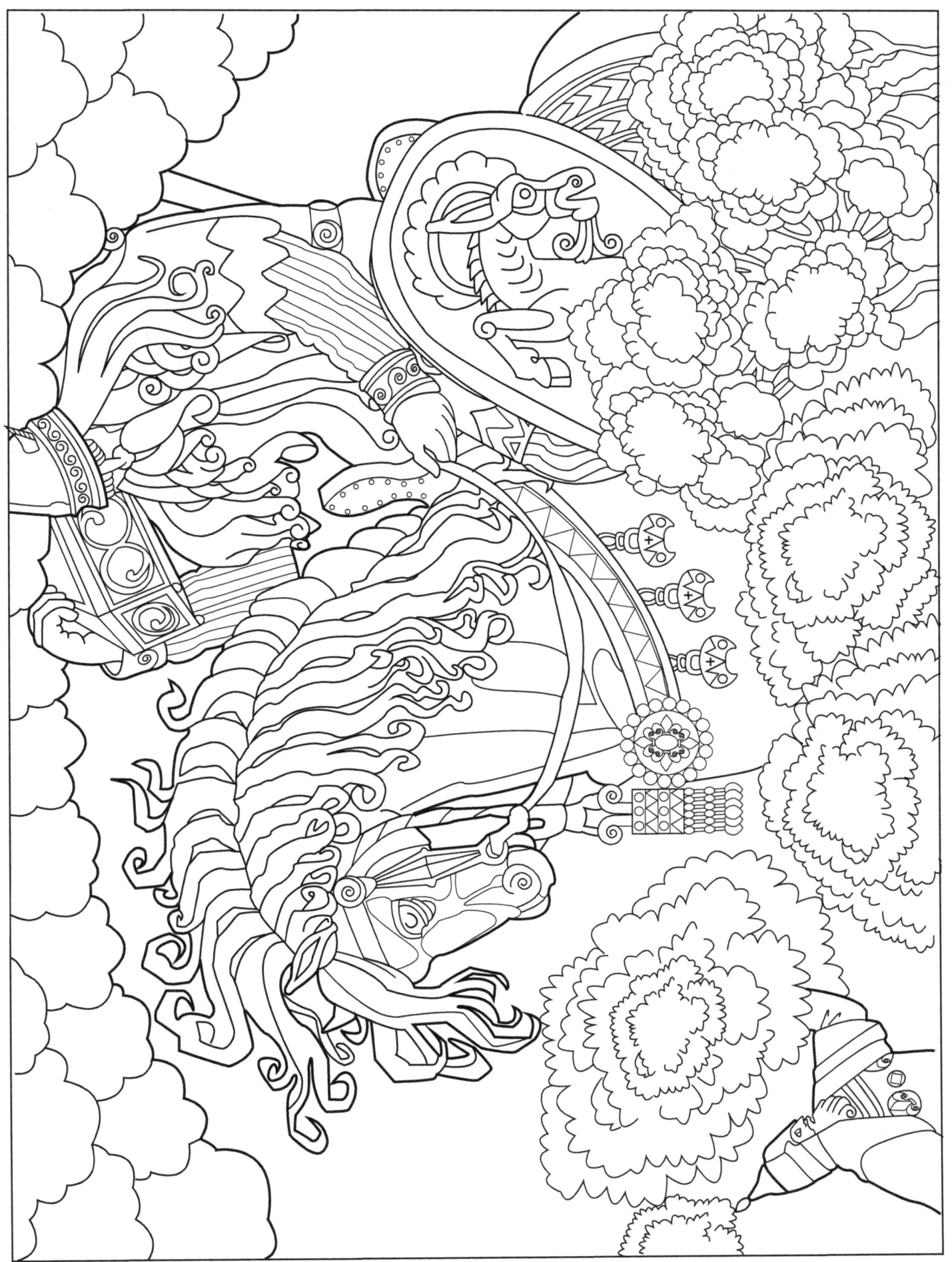

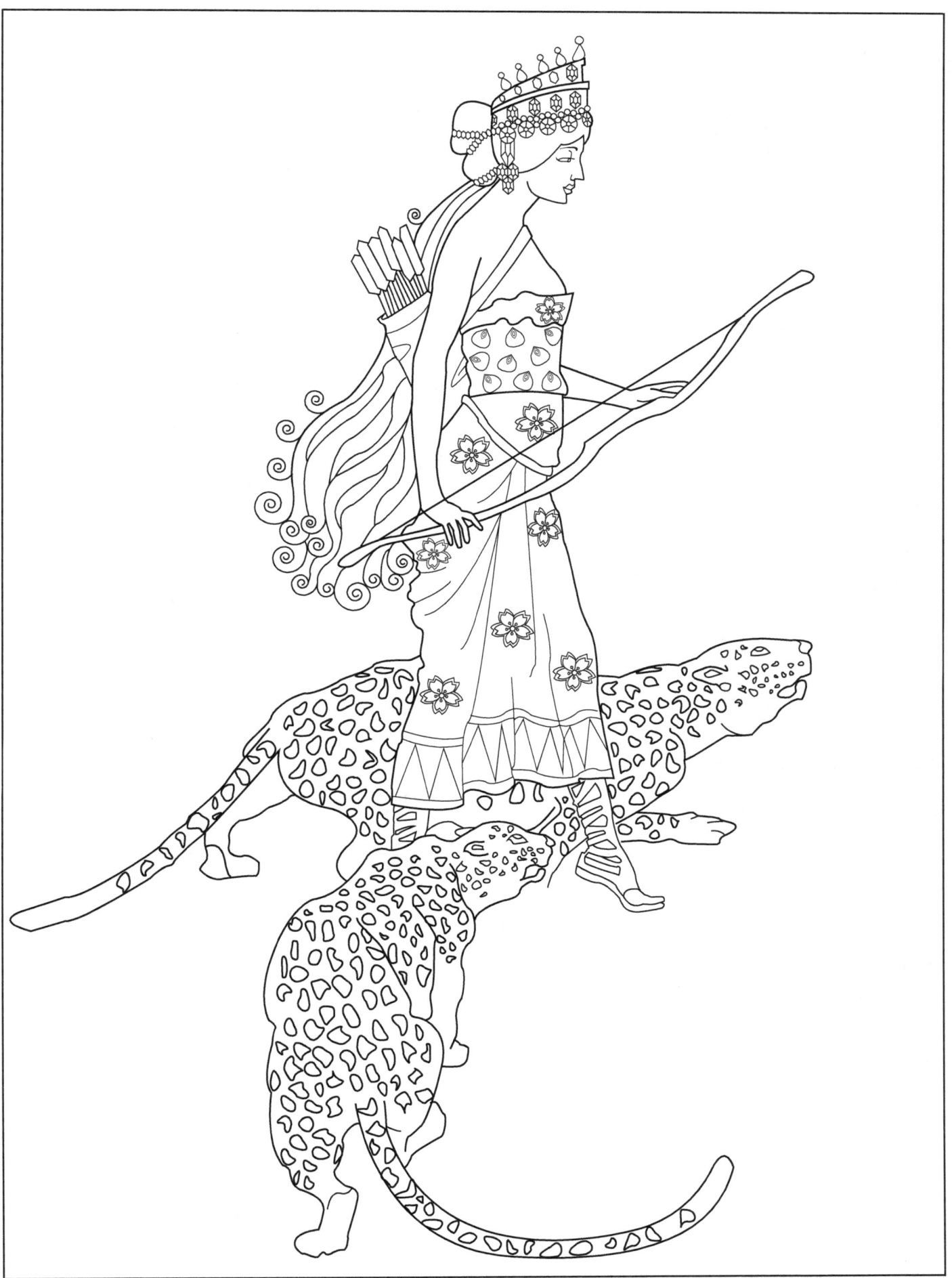

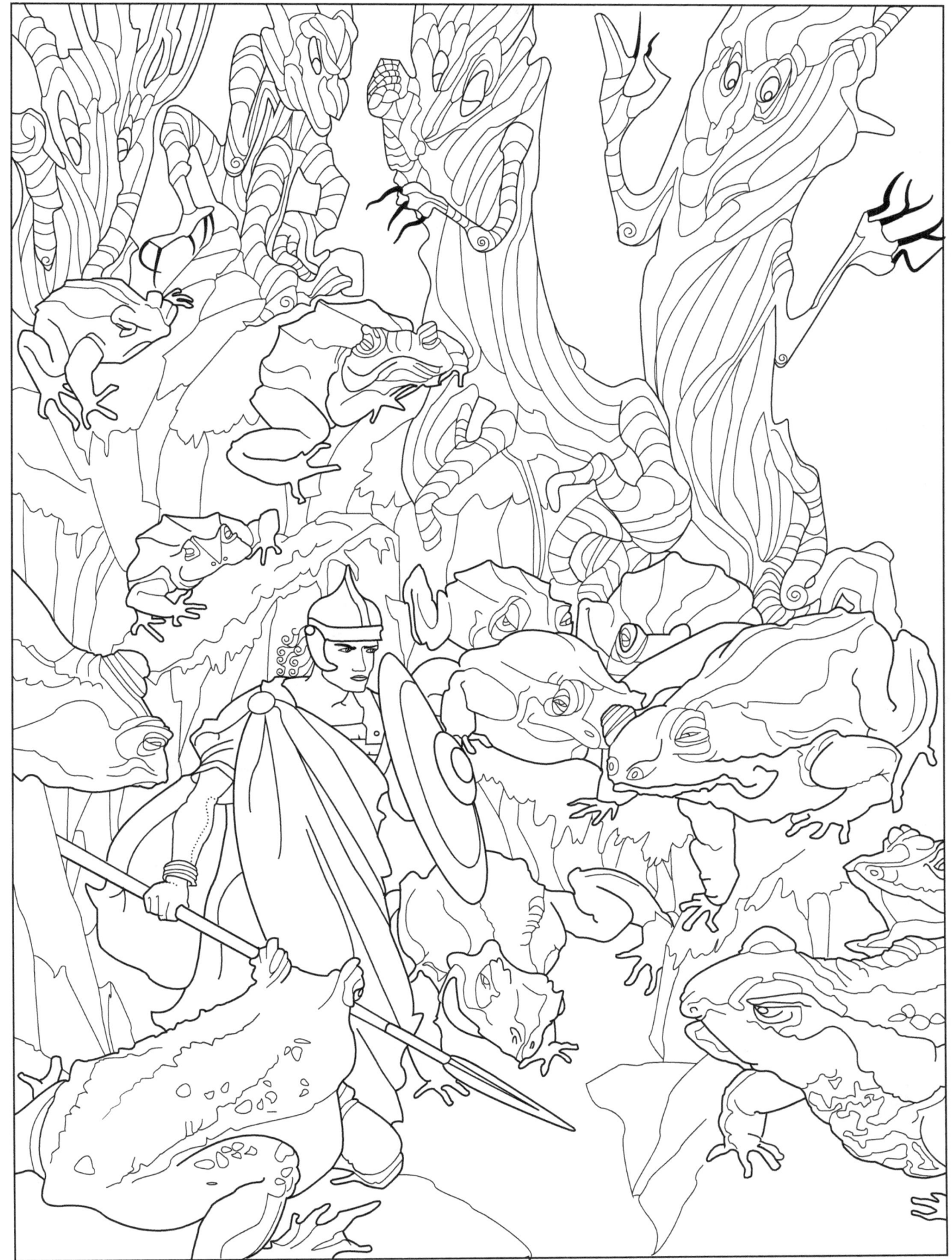

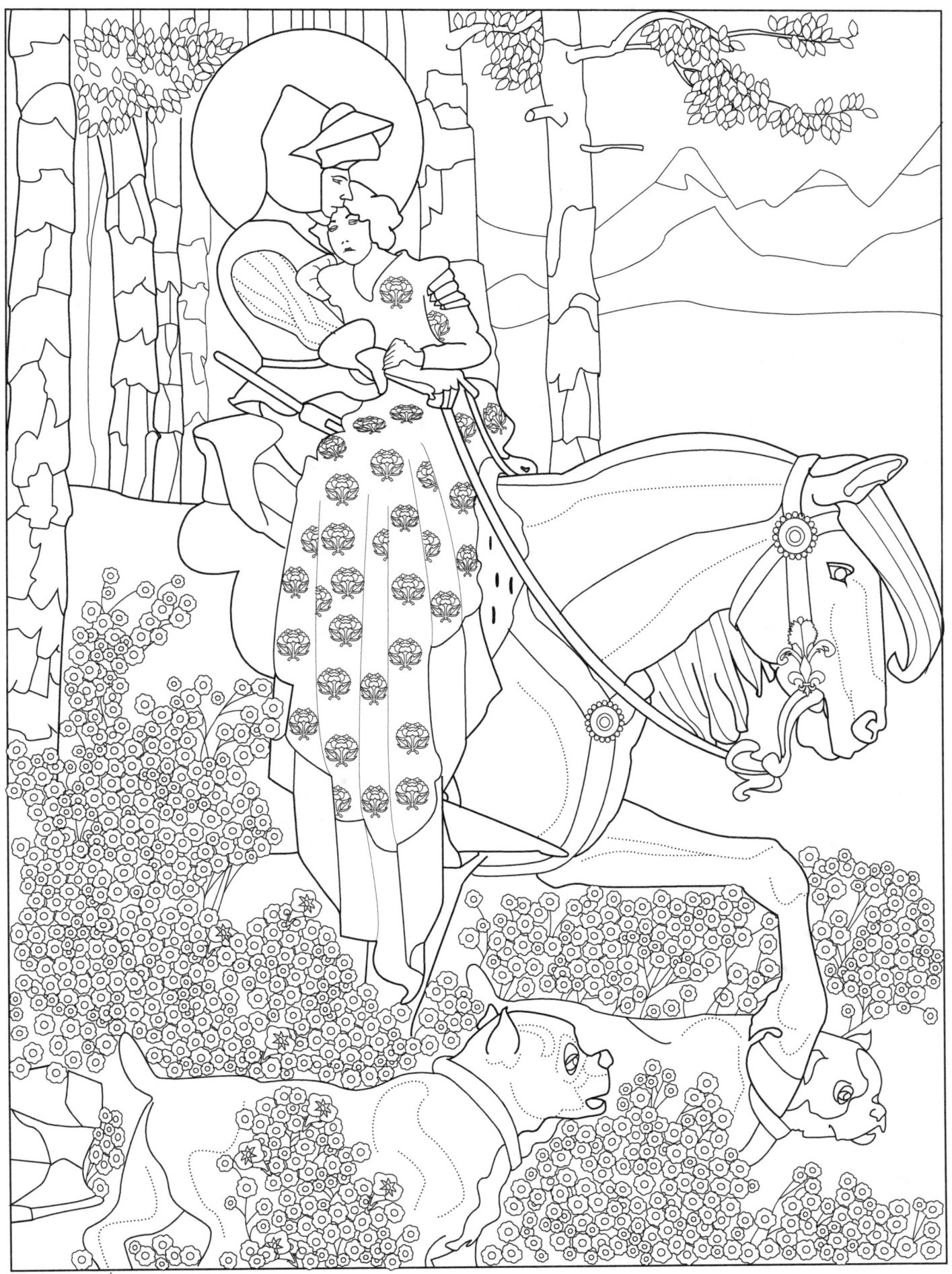

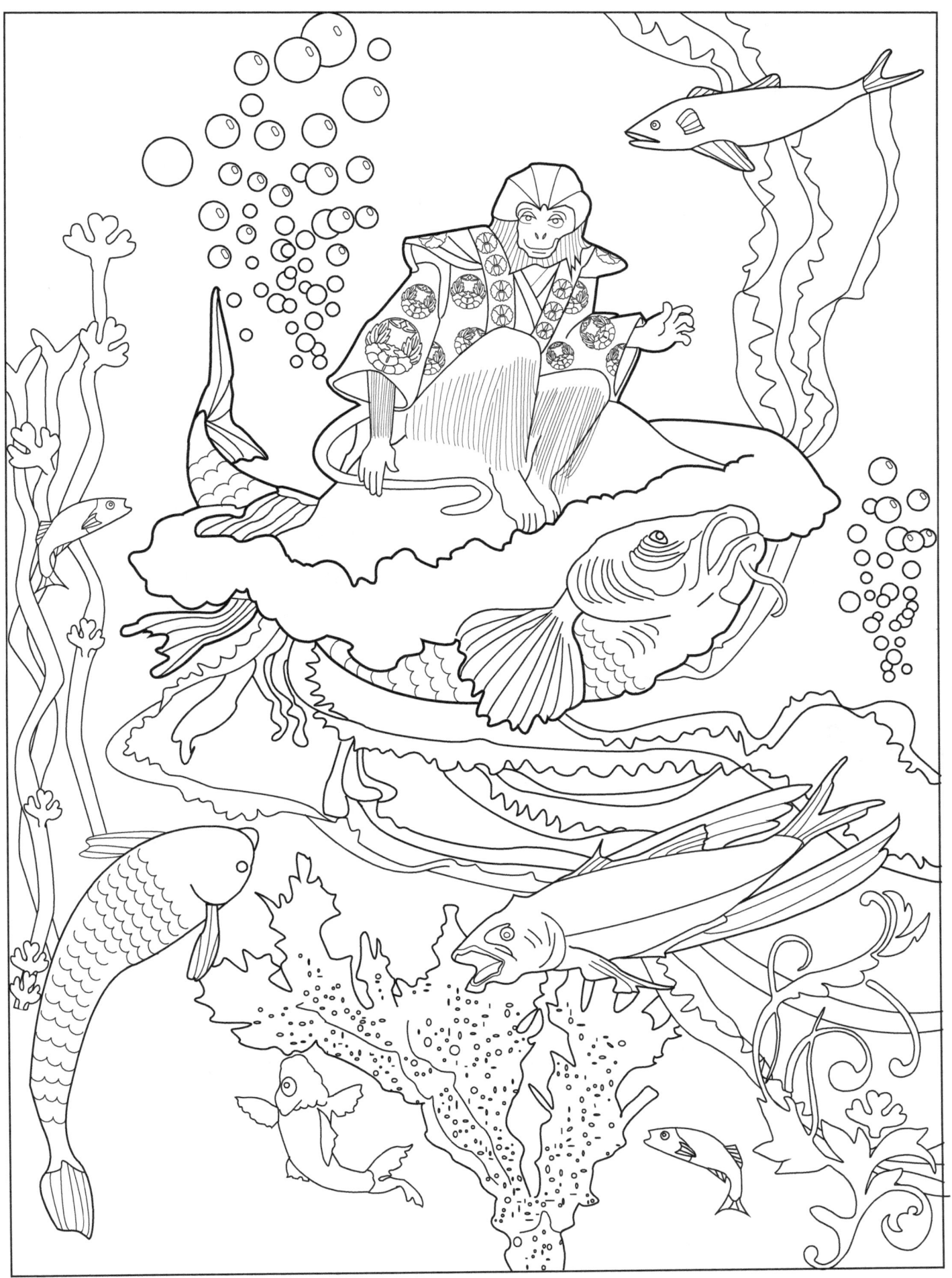

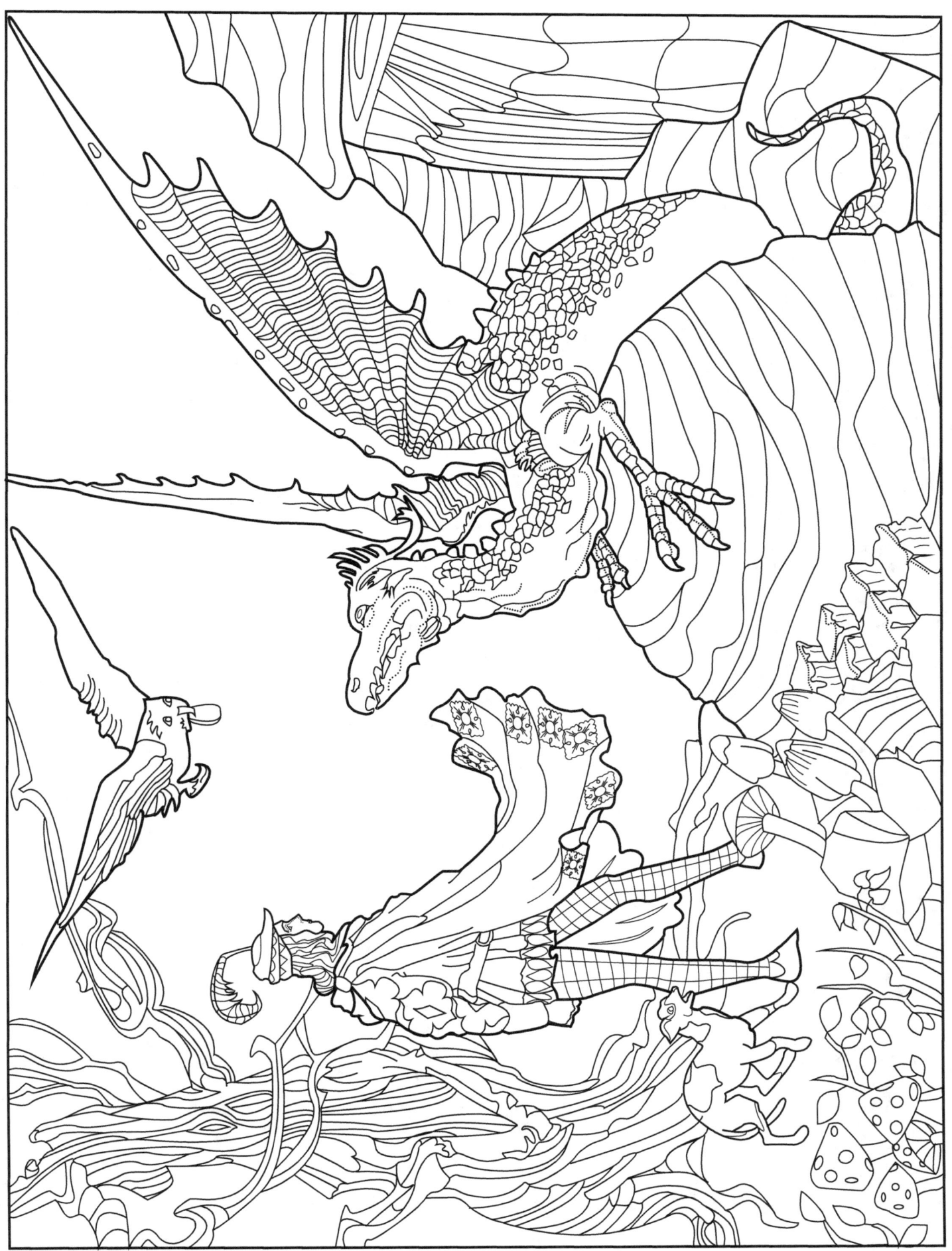

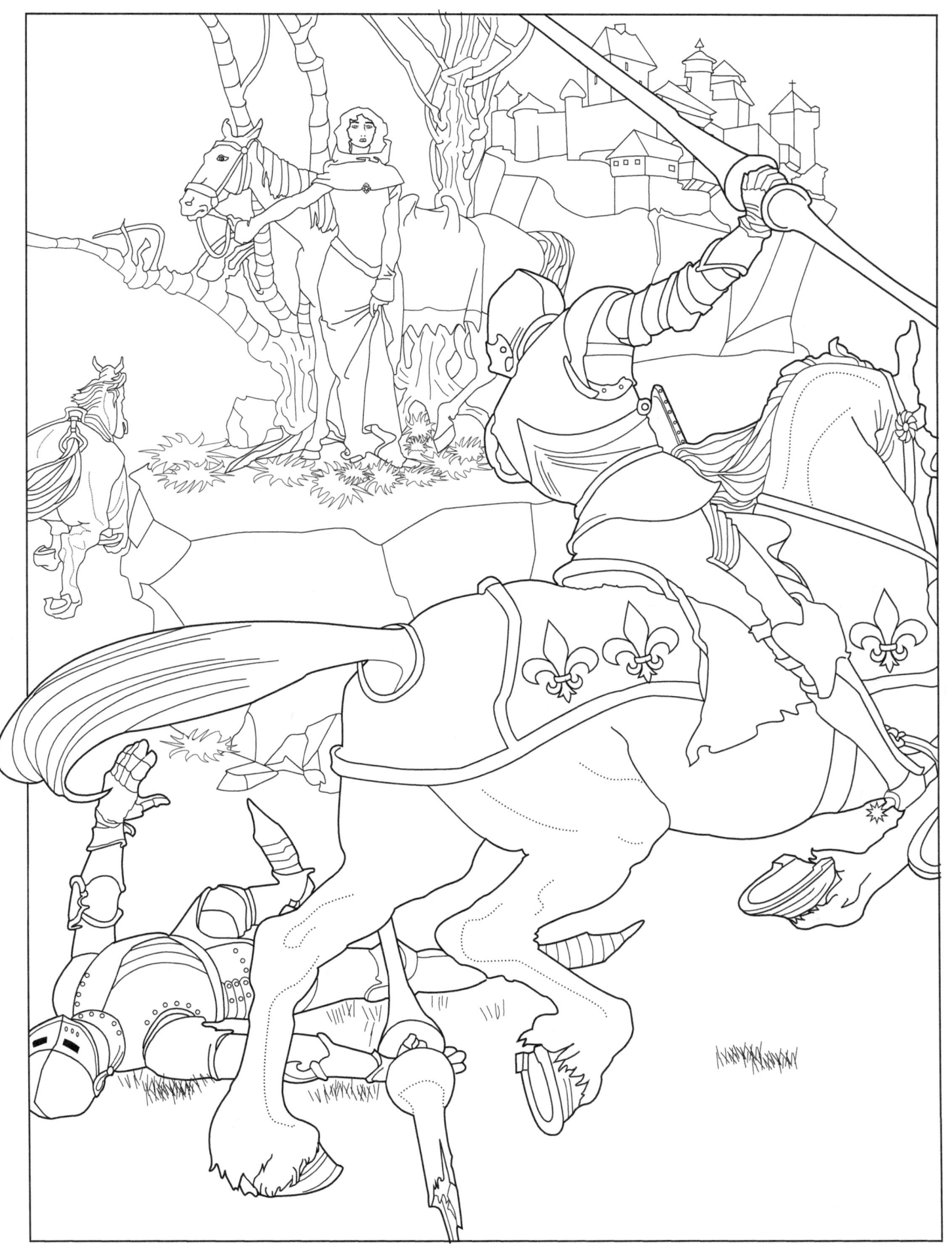

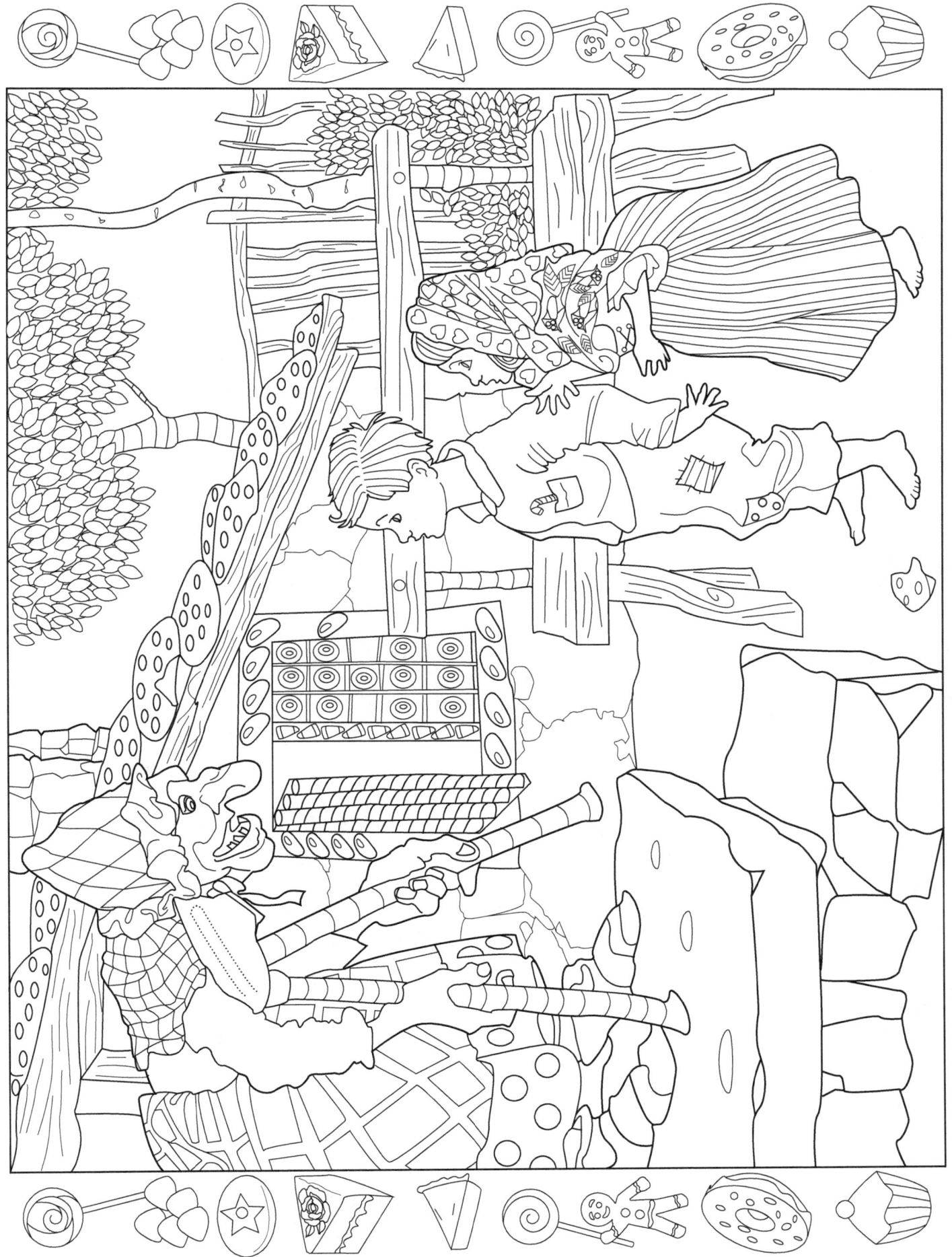

www.ingramcontent.com/pod-product-compliance
Lightning Source LLC
Chambersburg PA
CBHW081227170526
45165CB00009B/2979